Mrs. Nadine Clevenger

2001 Christmas

Shout to the Lord
Stories of God's Love and Power

INTEGRITY
BOOKS™

Tulsa, Oklahoma

Shout to the Lord
Stories of God's Love and Power
ISBN 1-57778-121-X
Copyright © 2001 by Integrity Incorporated
1000 Cody Road
Mobile, AL 36695

Published by ALBURY PUBLISHING
P. O. Box 470406
Tulsa, Oklahoma 74147

Original content produced by Marcia Ford, DeBary, Florida

DEDICATION

I would personally like to dedicate this book to a very exceptional young lady named Amy Newhouse. This beautiful girl inspired me more than she will ever know and I pray that the story of her life and testimony on page 42 will challenge you to live the life you've always imagined . . . giving glory to God with EVERY BREATH!

Darlene

CONTENTS

FOREWORD

And he hath put a new song in my mouth,

even praise unto our God: many shall see it,

and fear, and shall trust in the LORD.

—*Psalm 40:3 KJV*

When interviewers ask me to share the story behind my writing "Shout to the Lord," I have to say that it's not much of a story really. I didn't suddenly jump out of bed one morning and say to myself, "Oh! I think I'll write an incredible song that will touch the whole world!"

I think God just means some songs to be written. It's very embarrassing when people expect some big, dramatic story about a song God gave me in a time when I just needed to hear from Him. I was simply in the right place at the right time. I really feel that God should get the glory from sending this song to *all of us* when we needed it so much. It just happened to come out of my personal worship time with the Lord.

> *"Shout to the Lord" was born on one of those dark days in my life when I felt like everything was on top of me, threatening to crush me.*

I had been writing songs since I was 15, but I didn't even consider myself to be a songwriter. "Shout to the Lord" was born on one of those dark days in my life when I felt like everything was on top of me, threatening to crush me. There seemed to be no way out, and the only one I could turn to was the Lord. Desperate for His peace, I opened to the Psalms. I sat at our old out-of-tune piano tinkling the keys, and "Shout to the Lord" flowed out from my heart. I sang it over and over again and it lifted me up. Over the next few days, the song stayed with me, and it began to dawn on me that it might be a worship song.

I was terribly shy and felt a little embarrassed when I mentioned to Geoff Bullock, the Music Pastor, and Russell Fragar that I thought I had written a song. My hands were sweaty. I could hardly play it, I was so nervous. I kept starting and stopping. It took me twenty minutes to play it because I kept apologizing, "I'm sorry. Change anything you want. I know it's probably stupid." Eventually I made them stand with their backs to me while I played them the song. Even when they turned around and said that it was magnificent, I thought they were just being polite.

We introduced "Shout to the Lord" into our worship services and it began to spread from church to church. Before we had even recorded it, I began receiving thank-you letters from people all over the world who had sung the song in their churches.

I'm still amazed that when my pastor, Brian Houston, heard the song for the first time, he predicted it would be sung around the world. But when I remember that God is the One who gave the song, then I think perhaps I shouldn't be so surprised. Truly, the song's greatness comes from Him as all true praise does.

—Darlene

Shout to the Lord

My Jesus, My Savior,
Lord, there is none like You.
All of my days I want to praise
The wonders of Your mighty love.

My comfort, my shelter,
Tower of refuge and strength.
Let every breath, all that I am,
Never cease to worship You.

Shout to the Lord
All the earth, let us sing.
Power and majesty, praise to the King.
Mountains bow down and the seas will roar
At the sound of Your name.
I sing for joy at the work of Your hands,
Forever I'll love You, Forever I'll stand.
Nothing compares to the promise I have in You.

—Darlene Zschech

CHAPTER 1

My Jesus,
My Savior

My Jesus. How outrageous! To call Jesus "mine," just like "my neighbor" or "my co-worker." Why, that makes the Holy God seem so personal. But that's the Great News, isn't it? To be able to refer to the Creator God as your very own . . . friend, brother, helper, prayer partner, lover.

God has always craved personal relationships. He took nightly strolls with Adam through the garden. He ate a meal with Abraham. He even wrestled with Jacob. Jacob is amazed he lived through the wrestling match, not because of the physical pain but something more personal: "I saw God face to face, and yet my life was spared" (Genesis 32:30). Ours is a God who loves to have close contact with His creation.

Jesus presented Himself as personal. He invited fishermen into His life with two simple words, "Follow Me." "Get to know Me, get to know My ways," says Jesus. "I am not another idol, a statue, a block of wood. I am real, and I want you to get to know Me."

He invites us to join His family. "For whoever does the will of my Father in heaven is my brother and sister and mother" (Matthew 12:50). How much more personal can He get?

He lets us come with Him to a party. He allows us to see Him in despair. We watch Him play with children on His lap. We are witnesses as He casts moneychangers out of the Temple. Jesus does not hide Himself from us—we see Him up close and, yes, personal.

God, of course, already knows us far better than we know ourselves. "It is He who made us," the Psalmist says, "and we are his" (Psalm 100:3). God put all of our pieces together; He knows us inside and out. Even the secret parts of our heart that we think are hidden from view are visible to God. This is a very personal God indeed.

He is also my Savior, rescuing me from the fate I deserve. Jesus' sacrificial death is for all who believe, but only I can choose to accept this offer—undeserved life instead of well-deserved death—for my own life. Jesus truly is my Savior.

Even if I were the only person ever to sin, Jesus would have endured the cross to provide a means of salvation for me. We nod in agreement, but when we force our mind to comprehend this, the only genuine response must be one of humble thanksgiving. Jesus was willing to surrender all for just one person— even me.

Jesus loves to give eternal life to those who desire it; His purpose in coming to Earth was to give us this life. "I have come that they may have life, and have it to the full" (John 10:10). Here is Life Himself offering us the fullest life possible, free for the asking. Is there something inside of you wanting to shout right about now?

This gift of life is His to give, not ours to earn. Our only gift in return is a heart of thanksgiving, grateful that He is my Savior.

My Savior. Personal. He knows my name. He knows what I have—and haven't—done, and yet He thinks enough of me to leave the eternal throne room, take my place in death, and offer life in His pierced hand. This is our reason for singing, for laughing, for shouting. He is My Jesus.

Sing to the LORD,
praise his name;
proclaim his salvation
day after day.

Psalm 96:2

"I am the good
shepherd; I know
my sheep and my
sheep know me."

John 10:14

God Is Calling

Like lots of young people, Amanda thought God could wait for a while. After all, she wanted to have a good time, and it was just too hard to resist all the temptations that came her way. When I'm older, I won't have to face all this temptation, she reasoned. In the meantime, she would go to church, but she'd wait a while to clean up her act completely.

What she hadn't counted on was the relentless love of God. No matter what she did—no matter how sinful she perceived herself to be—there He was, beckoning her to give her life to Him.

The turning point in Amanda's understanding of the Christian life came at a music festival featuring the Hillsong singers. There, Amanda discovered that Christians could actually have fun, as she witnessed performers and festival-goers alike singing and laughing and shouting and having a great time together.

I hope God doesn't stop calling me, because I want so much for Him to be a part of my life one day.

Even better, Amanda learned a vital lesson—that she did not have to fix all the not-so-good stuff in her life in order to give herself to God. For the first time, she realized she could commit her life to the Lord first, and then He would help her resist temptation and clean up her act.

Her awareness of the love of the Lord was never stronger than when the group sang "Shout to the Lord." Although she sensed God's call more clearly than ever at that festival, something held her back from responding to Him. *I hope God doesn't stop calling me,* she thought, *because I want so much for Him to be a part of my life one day.*

By her own admission, Amanda is not quite there yet. She's closer, though—she finally understands that all she needs to do to experience salvation is to ask Jesus into her life. Right now, despite how easy it sounds, that's a difficult and scary prospect for her. But there's always hope for Amanda and others like her, that one day they will be able to sing, "My Jesus, my Savior."

"But I, when I am lifted up from the earth, will draw all men to myself."

—JOHN 12:32

CHAPTER 2

Lord, There Is None Like You

Imagine, for a moment, another God like the one we serve. You can't, can you? That's because He allows room for no other. As the all-knowing, all-powerful, ever-present one, He takes up all the space assigned to the name of God, and then some.

The prophet Jeremiah understood that truth completely, even as the nations surrounding the Israelites beckoned them to come on over and see what their gods could do. Their *gods*? Ha! says the prophet, comparing their idols to "a scarecrow in a melon patch" (Jeremiah 10:5). They can't speak, can't walk, can't do harm, can't do good. In a word, those other gods are worthless.

What about the God of the Bible, the one true Lord of the universe? Ah, now He's something to consider. Jeremiah coolly turns our attention toward Him in verse 6—"No one is like you, O LORD; you are great, and your

name is mighty in power"—and then cuts loose
through the rest of the chapter as he speaks of
the thundering presence of the Lord Almighty.
He leaves no doubt about it: No idol made
from a fallen tree or hammered metal is living
and active and responsive to the needs of those
who serve it; only the one true God, the eternal
King, is alive and active and ready—even
eager—to respond to those who love Him.

Centuries earlier, the psalmist, in expressing
his own awe of Yahweh, tried to make the
Israelites "get it" by emphasizing the uniqueness
of God, often in the form of a question:

Who is like You?

Who can compare with the Lord?

Who is like the Lord among the heavenly
beings?

Who is God besides the Lord?

Who is our Rock except our God?

Who, indeed? You can study other religions for a lifetime and never find a god who comes close to the God of the Bible. The very words we use to define Him fall far short of who He is. Knowing that, God gave us the ultimate Word— Jesus Christ, the Word who came to us in the form of a man. Even in His humanity, He showed us the incomparable nature of the Holy One; in His death, He revealed the matchless love of a Father who is like no other.

God, of course, has had His say about this all along. But seldom has He spoken more directly than He did when He asked the prophet Isaiah, *"To whom would you compare Me? Who would you say is My equal?"*

We know the answer. But with that answer comes a problem. If we know He is the only true God, if we have caught even a glimpse of His awesome power, how could we possibly treat Him with anything less than holy reverence? Who knows? We do it, though, all the time. And then, along He comes, drawing us into His forgiving embrace and loving us anyway—and once again, we are humbled by Almighty God. We simply cannot comprehend all that He is; there is nothing in our earthly frame of reference that can define or explain or encompass Him.

That's as it should be. To understand Him is to be Him, and that brings us right back to where we started from: Lord, there is none like You.

Among the gods
there is none like you,
O Lord; no deeds
can compare
with yours.

Psalm 86:8

Who has known the
mind of the Lord?
Or who has been his
counselor?

Romans 11:34

Opening Hearts to His Love

Something stirred in her heart as Beth boarded the plane bound for Central America. A sense of hope began welling up within her, a feeling she'd been lacking for some time. But lately, so many things in her life had been renewed and restored that Beth was beginning to get used to the changes. The fact that she was even on that plane is a testimony to the heart-changing power of the God who is like no other.

Months earlier, Beth had allowed her heart to be hardened by disappointments and had stopped caring deeply about anything, let alone missions. She half-heartedly agreed to attend a missions conference. As the participants prayed for missionaries in various countries, Beth stood under a large Guatemalan flag and began to intercede for the missionaries there. As she did, she began to have compassion not only for the missionaries but also for the people of Guatemala, even though she had never been to the Central American country. That night, God began to soften and renew her heart.

As the children began to sing and worship, Beth invited them to ask God to heal their hurt and tear down any walls they had placed around their hearts.

Sure enough, an opportunity arose for Beth to accompany a group of adults and teenagers from her church on a short-term missions trip to a children's home in Guatemala. They delivered supplies, helped with construction, ministered to the children, and conducted evangelistic outreach programs.

For an evening devotional with the children and staff, Beth talked about "Hearts and Flags" and explained how the group would use the small Guatemalan flags in the room as part of the praise and worship service. The flags, she said, symbolized a recent incident in her life when God changed her heart and gave her a love for the people of their country.

As the children began to sing and worship, Beth invited them to ask God to heal their hurt and tear down any walls they had placed around their hearts. She explained that while the walls may seem to protect them from pain, they also kept God's love at a distance. Waving the flags along with the music would show God that they were releasing their hurts and disappointments to Him and opening themselves up to His love.

To Beth, there could be no more beautiful sight than that of so many children and teens waving their flags as they sang "Canto al Señor," the Spanish-language version of "Shout to the Lord." Many of the children had come from heartbreaking backgrounds; some had mothers who were alive but couldn't support them. Even though the team's goal was to help the people of Guatemala, it was the missionaries who were the ones ministered to that night.

For weeks after returning home, Beth played "Shout to the Lord" over and over in her car. Although the stress in her life was nothing close to what those children had endured, the song helped her handle the troubling situations that confronted her at home. Now she sings along, with a smile on her face as she recalls the people of Guatemala.

The LORD will go forth like a warrior, He will arouse His zeal like a man of war. He will utter a shout, yes, He will raise a war cry. He will prevail against His enemies.

—ISAIAH 42:13 NASB

CHAPTER 3

All of My Days, I Want to Praise

Where does the desire to praise God come from? What causes our hearts to well up with cries of thanksgiving so that they overflow out of our mouths in shouts of praise?

Sometimes the wellspring of praise is primed by circumstance. We receive an unexpected financial blessing—just in time to pay a bill, buy a gift for a loved one, or to save for a rainy-day fund. We see an old friend who tells us he is now serving the Lord, in part due to our witness to him years ago. We are in love, and when we ask, she says "Yes!"

Perhaps we are in dire straits, desperately looking for a miracle. In times of great need, we look up to God and begin to praise Him for who we know Him to be. He is our Father, after all, and He will not forget about us. We know we are in His hand, and nothing can snatch us away from Him. In these times, our praise comes out quietly, but with an immense power that is beyond us.

Other times, that same well seems to have run dry. Oh, nothing is really wrong in our life—we just seem to be walking in the rut called "normal." It is in this period of walking out the daily life, when we are neither too high nor too low, we sometimes find praise difficult to give. But if we are to praise all of our days, including the normal ones, we must look beyond our own circumstances and emotions for our motivation.

One anchor of praise our souls can cling to is this: God never changes. He is the same yesterday, today and forever. The God we praised last month when we received that needed money? He is still here today when we are performing the mundane task of balancing the checkbook.

Remember how God provided a tow truck on that rainy day when our car stalled on a busy highway? He is right by our side today with the car full of kids—running just fine now, thank you—as we make the rounds to soccer and piano practices.

And that beautiful sunset last week, when we stood on the porch and praised God silently for being the most incredible artist ever? The same artist painted those clouds that have obscured the sun for the past three days.

But—here is the exciting part—the sun is still there. And so is God. He is not gone in our "rut" times. And when we choose to offer our praise to Him, even when we don't particularly feel like it, it is amazing how "sunny" we begin to feel. God truly inhabits the praises of His people. When you start to sing, recite Psalms, or speak out His greatness, you cannot keep Him from flooding your life right then and there!

He is deserving and desirous of our praise all of our days—the great ones, the terrible ones, and even the average ones.

My Jesus,

My Saviour

*I will praise you
as long as I live, and
in your name I will
lift up my hands.*

Psalm 63:4

*Lord there is none
like You.*

Through Jesus,
therefore, let us
continually offer to
God a sacrifice of
praise——the fruit
of lips that confess
his name.

Hebrews 13:15

Amy's Legacy

Even as a young child, Amy Newhouse was different from other kids. By the time she reached her teens, her passion for Jesus had clearly set her apart. Her heart's desire was to spread the news of Christ to students at her high school in Pampa, Texas. For Amy, this was not an act. Her love for God was real.

At times, being different was tough on her—as when the other kids would taunt her about her faith and the pledge of purity she had made or exclude her from parties and other activities. For the most part, she took it all in stride and prayed that God would bless her friends, but at other times her disappointment and hurt showed.

Sensing the respect that Amy's friends had for her despite their outward actions, Amy's mother encouraged her to lean on God for the strength to maintain her convictions. By living out her beliefs and never wavering from her faith in Christ, Amy was influencing her peers more than she would ever know.

As always, the Father offered just the right treatment, at just the right time.

In January of 1999, Amy was diagnosed with non-Hodgkins Lymphoma, which was already well advanced by the time her doctor detected it. As the doctor broke the news to Amy and her parents, carefully explaining the seriousness of the situation, Amy said, "Well, praise God! I have been praying for God to use me in a mighty way to bring my friends to Christ. And if this is what it takes, then praise God!"

"Honey, that's a wonderful thing to say, but do you realize we are talking about your life here?" her father asked.

"Well, duh!" she responded, her huge smile revealing her wonderfully deep dimples. From that day on, Amy had peace about her illness.

The treatments were hard on her body. The cancer had progressed rapidly, and she was subjected to large doses of chemotherapy. In February, she developed mucositis, a disintegration of the mucous lining of the gastrointestinal tract. Sores the size of a thumbnail covered her lips, mouth, tongue, and throat. The physician said her internal system was a solid wall of bleeding, oozing sores. No matter the dosage, pain medication failed to give her any real relief.

What did provide a measure of relief was the music she listened to in her room in the hospital's intensive care unit. She would play "Shout to the Lord" over and over, with her mother often leaning over her and singing along. As that song ministered to Amy's spirit, a peace would fall over her face, and she would experience temporary relief from the pain. As always, the Father offered just the right treatment, at just the right time.

In September of 1999, five days before her seventeenth birthday, Amy joined her Father in heaven. But before she did, she discovered that her life had touched not only her friends but also casual acquaintances and others who had never met her. To this day, her family hears from people whose lives she touched and who were led to the cross because of her example.

Don't worry about anything, but pray about everything. With thankful hearts offer up your prayers and requests to God. Then, because you belong to Christ Jesus, God will bless you with peace that no one can completely understand. And this peace will control the way you think and feel.

—PHILIPPIANS 4:6-7 CEV

CHAPTER 4

The Wonders of Your Mighty Love

Have you ever stopped to imagine just what are these wonders of His mighty love? We could try listing them—but that would take eternity, especially since there's little likelihood we'd ever find the words that could adequately describe His love. Or we could point to biblical examples of the power of His love: from the creation of our incredible world to the mercy shown to a motley crew of fishermen.

Then there are the wonders we've seen in our own world: a weeping father brought to the throne of grace, finally set free from the bondage of alcohol; a sexually abused friend finding peace and healing in the tender embrace of the Lord; a tiny European nun bringing hope to the diseased and homeless and unloved in India.

We have many opportunities each day to see the wonders of His mighty love. But there is one Wonder that surpasses all others. One evidence of His mighty love that stands so far apart from all else that it is the very definition of love itself: Jesus Christ, nailed to a cross, dying so we might live.

"This is love: not that we loved God, but that he loved us and sent his Son as an atoning sacrifice for our sins." Make no mistake about it, the apostle John tells us in his first letter (4:10)—*this is love*. John, the disciple whom Jesus loved, would be one to know.

Love is the blood streaking down the face of our Lord as the crown of thorns is pushed onto His head. Love is the scars on His back left by a lead-tipped whip. Love is the water and blood gushing from His pierced side.

Love is the Father placing the burden of sin on the shoulders of His Son so we would no longer have to bear it ourselves.

That, the apostle Paul wrote in the letter we call Romans, is exactly how God chose to demonstrate His love for us. He allowed His Son to die for us *while we were still sinners* (5:8). We didn't have to get our act together before we came to the cross. He didn't require us to take a drug test or go twenty-four hours without lying or apologize to anyone for anything. No, all we had to do was come.

There, at the foot of the cross, His mighty Love would meet us. And there we would find the power and the strength to begin life all over again, this time *knowing* that we're loved. We were always loved, of course, but we didn't know it. We *couldn't* know it because we didn't know God. And knowing God, we now know love—because God is love.

That's a lot to take in. No wonder the wisdom of God appears to be foolishness to those outside His family of believers. If we hadn't experienced all this for ourselves—if we hadn't danced for joy after first crawling to the cross—well, we'd no doubt find all this pretty hard to believe.

When you come right down to it, it's *all* a wonder.

Show the wonder of your great love, you who save by your right hand those who take refuge in you...

Psalm 17:7

For I am convinced
that neither death nor
life, neither angels nor
demons, neither the
present nor the future,
nor any powers, neither
height nor depth, nor
anything else in all
creation, will be able to
separate us from the love
of God that is in Christ
Jesus our Lord.

Romans 8:37,38

A Song of Healing

David George stood quietly before the congregation at Bread of Life Church in Houston, Texas. Next to him stood the senior pastor, Dusty Kemp, whom David had served as an associate pastor for the previous year and a half. But on this day, David eyed Dusty anxiously, only vaguely aware of who he was. The unfamiliar church was filled with people who were now strangers to him.

The date was July 30, 2000, and no one in the service could have predicted the worldwide impact David's presence that day would eventually have. Three weeks earlier, the assistant pastor had swerved his car to avoid missing a pedestrian and suffered a serious brain injury resulting in significant memory loss and slowed speech. The prognosis was that he would recover only eighty percent of his brain function following nearly a year of intense therapy.

Following a time of praise and worship, Pastor Dusty updated the congregation on David's condition and handed him a microphone,

> "When we were singing 'Shout to the Lord' ... something began to rise, and I could feel God coming down as we praised Him with a loud voice. Something began to happen around here. Chains broke . . ."

hoping he would be able to say a few words. At first he stammered and paused several times to pull himself together.

Finally, he was able to express himself: "When we were singing 'Shout to the Lord' ... something began to rise, and I could feel God coming down as we praised Him with a loud voice. Something began to happen around here. Chains broke . . ." David stopped suddenly, looked around the church, and stared up at the dome. "Boy! . . . *He's* here!"

Suddenly, David realized that not only was he talking, but also he no longer felt the back pain that had plagued him since the accident. What's more, he began to single out people in the congregation, identifying them by name. The tears began to flow as David was being healed, mentally and physically, right before their eyes. The front of the church began to fill with weeping people who came to kneel before Jesus and worship Him.

The following Tuesday, David went for the first session of what was to be a five-hour-a-day rehabilitation program, expected to last six months. After his initial exam for the treatment, the doctors were astounded by his improvement. They would have pronounced him fully recovered, but they couldn't believe it. They did manage to tell him he did not need therapy. Then they sent him home.

If not for the goodness of God, Pastor David would have had to endure nearly a full year of therapy. Instead, he began an intensive traveling schedule, for a very good cause: The entire service in which he was healed was captured on videotape, and copies of the tape have been sent to hundreds of churches and thousands of individuals in more than twenty-six countries. He shares his story whenever and wherever he can, testifying to the wonders of the mighty love of God.

> *Oh, the depth of the riches both of the wisdom and knowledge of God! How unsearchable are His judgments, and unfathomable His ways!*

> —ROMANS 11:33 NASB

CHAPTER 5

My Comfort,
My Shelter

There was a popular poster available in bookstores in the 1970s. It showed a boat safely tied up to a dock, with blue skies behind it. The caption on the poster read, "A ship in the harbor is safe—but that is not what ships are built for."

Taking a ship out of the safety of the harbor can be a dangerous undertaking. Out at sea are storms, underwater structures that remain unseen until it is too late, and the possibility of losing one's bearings so that the ship becomes lost. With such terrible circumstances very real, why would anyone take the risk of putting out to sea when the harbor offers shelter and safety?

The answer, of course, is that ships are made for the seas, not for the harbor.

The same can be said for our lives. We are made for adventure, not for "playing it safe." But—here is the exciting part!—our Shelter is always with us. We have a constant Refuge to run to.

Let's look at some biblical examples. Abram was called to leave the safety of his family and the land he knew as his home. He was to go where God directed him, one step at a time. This was very risky—he took his wife away from her family shelter as well. Yet God was with them throughout their journey, protecting, providing, guiding. Abram could not have become Abraham, the father of God's chosen people, if he had elected to remain in his "harbor."

Ruth could have stayed in her hometown, among her people and her gods. She was under no obligation to go with her mother-in-law, Naomi. After all, Ruth's husband—Naomi's son—was dead. But Ruth chose to return with Naomi to Naomi's homeland. And there God provided a shelter in the person of Boaz, who protected Ruth and Naomi, eventually taking

Ruth as his bride. This union led to the birth of Israel's great King David.

In the earliest days after the resurrection of Jesus, Peter and John had to decide whether to play it safe, or to obey God. Brought before the religious and legal leaders of their day, Peter and John were ordered to stop preaching in the name of Jesus. But these two disciples knew their true Shelter existed in sailing the seas of God. They chose obedience to God over obedience to men, and found comfort in God's protection.

The Psalmist writes in Psalm 107:23-24, "Those who go to the sea in ships, who do business on great waters, they have seen the works of the LORD, and His wonders in the deep" (NASB). We cannot see the great works of God in the shallow waters—we must venture out from the safety of the harbor in the deep waters. There we will see God's majesty, and we will come to know Him as our Comfort and our

Shelter in ways we could never know if we stayed near the shore.

He who dwells in the
shelter of the Most
High will rest in
the shadow of
the Almighty.

Psalm 91:1

Praise be to the God
and Father of our
Lord Jesus Christ,
the Father of
compassion and the
God of all comfort,
who comforts us in
all our troubles...

2 Corinthians 1:3,4

Heavenly Greeters

It was the worst news a pregnant woman could receive—the baby she was carrying had a heart defect so serious that he stood no chance of survival. Theresa and Dan let the tears flow as they left the doctor's office and headed for the home of Theresa's older sister, Kate.

Though both sisters had given their lives to the Lord as children, only Kate still had a relationship with Him. When Theresa and her husband arrived at Kate's house that day, Theresa fell into her sister's arms, sobbing and asking her to pray for them. Kate prayed one of the most difficult prayers of her life, asking God for healing, peace, comfort, wisdom, and strength.

Theresa's doctor advised her to abort the baby, explaining that he would induce labor, allow the baby to be born, and let him die. But one night, Dan had a powerful dream. In it, he held a baby boy, looked into his eyes, and was overwhelmed with love for him. They cancelled the appointment they had made for the abortion.

Kate prayed one of the most difficult prayers of her life, asking God for healing, peace, comfort, wisdom, and strength.

While still in his mother's womb, Steven, as they had named their unborn son, began to show signs of improvement. Even so, he was not expected to live. Within a week of his birth, Steven underwent the first of three heart operations. After seven months of hospital stays, Steven was able to go home.

Then one weekend, Steven's condition worsened. It was clear that he was dying. Not knowing what else to do, Kate bought a gift for Theresa—the *Shout to the Lord* CD. For the rest of the day, the Hillsong music brought the peace of God into a house that had been filled with grief.

That night, Steven gave up his fight for life. At that moment, Kate heard a child's voice calling Steven's name, as if a friend was greeting him joyfully after he'd been away. Meanwhile, just before Steven died, Theresa had briefly fallen asleep and dreamed she saw three children jumping up and down, welcoming Steven into heaven, but she couldn't hear what they were saying. Kate told her what she had heard.

Immediately, the Spirit of God fell on Theresa. She marched out of the bedroom and put on the CD Kate had bought. The entire house filled up with God's Spirit. The heaviness left, and the two sisters fell on their knees and worshiped God. Theresa gathered the entire family together and prayed for the strength to make it through the days ahead, releasing her son to Jesus.

Kate and Theresa are convinced they know who was waiting for Steven on the other side.

This was not Theresa's first pregnancy; she had lost her first child to miscarriage. Kate had also lost her first child to miscarriage—and had miscarried her second child, a girl who would have been born around the same time Steven was. Three miscarriages, three children—ready and waiting to welcome Steven into heaven.

You have turned for me my mourning into dancing;

You have loosed my sackcloth and girded me with gladness;

That my soul may sing praise to You and not be silent.

O LORD my God, I will give thanks to You forever.

—PSALM 30:11,12 NASB

CHAPTER 6

Tower of Refuge and Strength

Of all the people whose stories are recorded in the Bible, no one had a better understanding of God as a refuge than David did. We might have a few enemies here and there, but David had an entire army in hot pursuit of him alone. We could learn a thing or two from such a man.

Look at one of the songs he wrote, this one recorded in 2 Samuel 22:2-3:

"The LORD is my rock, my fortress and my

deliverer;

my God is my rock, in whom I take refuge,

my shield and the horn of my salvation,

He is my stronghold, my refuge and my

savior—

from violent men you save me."

At the time David wrote this, he had no way of knowing how many more times in his life he would have to seek refuge in the Lord. Having escaped certain death at the hands of Saul, David must have thought the worst was behind him. But over and over, through military battles and family upheaval and moral failure, David ran to the Tower of Refuge and Strength that is the Lord.

Our problems are not the same as David's, but they are real nonetheless. Relatives mock us, a business partner deceives us, children dishonor us, our spouse abandons us. Then, too, it's not just people but also the overwhelming pressures of daily life that send us looking for a way out. Unpaid bills, unreliable cars, leaking roofs, and medical emergencies can create an enormous amount of stress, especially in a single-parent household. No, we're not ducking actual spears and arrows, but sometimes it feels as if we are.

Maybe it would help if we update the language a bit here, as Eugene Peterson has done in The Message. In Psalm 9:9, he calls God a "safe-house for the battered." Now that's an image straight out of contemporary life. A woman is beaten by an abusive husband; she fears for the life of her children. Frantically, the woman seeks out help and finds it in a safe-house, a place where she and her children are hidden away and shielded from the one intent on doing them harm.

That's the kind of place God can be for us, once we've learned to run to Him in prayer. As He enfolds His loving and protective arms around us, He becomes as a safe-house to us. We are secure, hidden from view, and locked away from those who would attack us. He is our strength in our time of greatest weakness and vulnerability.

It doesn't matter whether the attacks are verbal or physical, psychological or emotional. God is the same, yesterday, today, and forever. He wants us to call on Him as David did, so He can be for us our Rock and our Deliverer.

*God is our refuge
and strength,
an ever-present
help in trouble.*

Psalm 46:1

But the Lord is
faithful, and he will
strengthen and
protect you from
the evil one.

2 Thessalonians 3:3

"I Want You to Praise Me"

Clay Basington was well on his way to becoming a bona fide workaholic. For years he had done everything in his power to have an effective ministry, leading worship services, choirs, and youth groups. Nothing seemed to work for him.

One night, Clay awoke in agonizing pain. Medical tests conducted over the next few weeks revealed nothing conclusive. For two months, Clay remained bedridden, leaving the house only for more testing.

Believers prayed for his recovery; church elders anointed him with oil. Nothing happened—except to Clay's faith, which plummeted to an all-time low. Not only did he question God's failure to heal him, he also found himself tempted to question His very existence. Through months of prayer and Bible reading, he regained his faith, but Clay was still in excruciating pain.

Assured that he was now right with God, Clay settled back and waited to die.

Convinced he was about to die, he accused God of being unfair, especially after all Clay had done for Him. *I shouldn't be treated this way!* Clay thought, insisting that God answer for Himself. It was not a moment Clay was proud of, but it was an honest one.

Had he known how God would answer, Clay no doubt would have bit his tongue. "Clay, I've seen all the things you have been doing, and they are good things," he sensed God say to him. "The only problem is that I am not in them. You are doing it all yourself. And furthermore, Clay, I don't need you."

Shaken to the very core of his being, Clay began to weep, confessing his sins, repenting, and seeking God's forgiveness. Assured that he was now right with God, Clay settled back and waited to die. But he didn't. Instead, he re-committed his life to God and vowed to do whatever God asked of him—this time, in God's power and not his own.

"I want you to praise Me," God said.

Clay began to argue that he was in too much pain to sing, but figuring that he was going to lose that argument anyway, he began to sing to the Lord. By his own admission, his effort was pitiful. "There's no way that I can, with any integrity, praise You for how I feel," he eventually told God. "I'm really hurting. Have You ever hurt like this?"

With those words, Clay saw Jesus hanging on the cross. After Clay finished yet another round of confession, repentance, and prayer for forgiveness, the Lord reminded him that he was to praise Him for who He is, not for his own healing. Chastened again, Clay began to sing songs about the greatness of God and His character. For the first time, he knew how it felt to worship God in spirit and in truth. An hour later, Clay stood up—and as he did, the pain fell away from him. In an instant, Clay was healed—and the Southern Baptist pastor began dancing and leaping for joy before the Lord. Praise had brought on his healing.

Give thanks in all circumstances, for this is God's will for you in Christ Jesus.

—1 THESSALONIANS 5:18

CHAPTER 7

Let Every Breath, All That I Am

I surrender all. That's what we're saying to God when we lose ourselves in worship to Him. With every breath, with every fiber of our being, we offer ourselves as a sacrifice of praise and worship. God calls us to Himself, and, like the patriarchs of the faith, we answer, "Here I am." Take every part of me, every blessed bit, because I am nothing apart from You.

In our surrender, though, we have to include the stuff we bring along with us—the good, the bad, and the ugly. Our dreams, our hopes, our desires—those can all be good things, but they still have to go on the altar of surrender. The bad? Where do we begin with that? The ugly— those hidden sins that are so hideous that we don't even want to look at them, let alone expose them to the light of God's presence.

The wonderful old hymn "I Surrender All" reminds us that we must freely give all those things we delight in that are not of God: "All to

Jesus I surrender; humbly at his feet I bow, worldly pleasures all forsaken; take me, Jesus, take me now." There's a payoff, of course, as there always is with God, and the scales are always tipped to give us "exceedingly and abundantly," to use a biblical phrase, far more than we can ever hope to offer Him. As we surrender, we receive His power and blessing and even "the sacred flame...the joy of full salvation." The hymn writer, one J.W. Van Deventer, had it right: The joy of our salvation, when we experience it to its fullest, burns hot within us, fueled by the Holy Spirit's presence as we worship the Lord.

To keep that sacred flame burning requires day by day surrender of all that we are. Unless we approach the Lord in absolute truth and honesty, we shortchange ourselves *and* Him. We know what we're holding back, and He's well aware of our deception. Our lack of openness blocks genuine intimacy with the Father.

And isn't intimacy what we're after? Then why do we do the very things that prevent us from experiencing it? God wants to share an intimate relationship with us even more than we want one with Him—so much so that He gives us the power and ability to make intimacy possible. We love to complicate the things of God, but in this case, the remedy is simple: Confess and renounce those things that are preventing true intimacy, accept His guaranteed forgiveness, and joyfully step into His presence.

Now that we've *given up* the sin that so easily entangles us, it's time for us to get busy with our *giving*. Give our heart, so He can make it whole. Give our mind, so He can renew it. Give our spirit, so He can refresh it. Give our body, so He can energize it. Give it all to Him— simply because.

He has given us every breath we'll ever take. Our very life is contained in each breath, and right now, He knows how many more breaths each one of us has left.

No matter what is holding you back, give it up. Give Him every breath, all that you are, the very life He gave you—give it all back to Him in worship and adoration.

*Let everything
that has breath praise
the LORD.*

Psalm 150:6

"As surely as I
live," says the Lord,
"every knee will
bow before me;
every tongue will
confess to God."

Romans 14:11

Rescued for a Reason

The news broke about midday June 29, 1996, that a fishing boat had sunk in deep water eight miles off the coast of North Queensland, Australia. Two fishermen were presumed drowned, and three others were lost at sea.

The first survivor to be rescued was Pastor Tim Edwards, who had spent fifteen hours in the water before the Coast Guard found him clinging to a buoy. From Tim they learned that two men—Tim's younger brother David and brother-in-law Tom—had drowned in the raging sea, Tom crying out for the Lord to take him into His presence peacefully and David crying, "Lord Jesus, save me!" Neither man could swim.

Another man, Alex, held on to his 14-year-old son Nathan, the only one of the five who was wearing a life jacket. Trying to stay afloat as the wind and waves battered them, Tim joined Alex and Nathan in singing "Amazing Grace." Soon, though, the elements separated Tim from the others. He was now alone in his fight for survival.

A single line from "Shout to the Lord"— "Let every breath all that I am/Never cease to worship You"—kept him going all day.

Trusting the Holy Spirit for the strength to swim, Tim spent ten hours in cold, deep, rough seas, singing songs and saying endless prayers. A single line from "Shout to the Lord"— "Let every breath all that I am/Never cease to worship You"—kept him going all day.

In the fading light, he caught a glimpse of a buoy off in the distance, his only hope for a much-needed rest after swimming for so many hours. Night came quickly, but the beacon light on the buoy guided Tim's way. When he finally reached the buoy, he climbed up on it, but the air was too cold. For the next six hours, he held onto the buoy but remained in the water, feeling hypothermia set in. In the middle of the night, he saw a Coast Guard vessel several miles away, obviously searching for the missing fishermen.

"Lord, it's a miracle that I've survived this long," Tim prayed. "I ask you for another miracle. Please send that boat directly to where I am."

Within no time, the boat reached him, and he was pulled safely on board. The following day, Alex and Nathan were rescued by a fishing trawler after eighteen hours at sea.

Thousands of Christians around Australia had prayed for the safe return of the survivors. For Tim, losing Tom and David was a tragedy that he could not have handled without the ministry of the Comforter, the Holy Spirit. Even as he fought the stormy sea to stay alive, the praises he sang to God, with every breath that he had, brought peace even in the midst of tragedy. Today, Tim Edwards understands grief and sorrow as he never has before—but he's also seen God turn his grief and sorrow into joy and dancing.

Help us, O God of our salvation, for the glory of thy name.

—PSALM 79:9 KJV

CHAPTER 8

Never Cease to Worship You

Ceaseless, never-ending worship sounds nice, but just how can you do it? How can praise become such an ingrained part of your life that you never stop?

Think of it as a supernatural form of multitasking. When you're praying, you're also worshiping God, right? And when you're singing a psalm to God, that's like a lyrical prayer—which is a form of worship—which is...well, you get the point.

The problem here stems from our misunderstanding of the word *worship*. Yes, worship is something we do in a church service or in a cell group or at a Christian music festival. That kind of worship involves singing and—if we're really uninhibited—dancing before the Lord. It's most often a time in the event when a reverential tone settles over the people.

Experiencing true worship in a group setting requires the ability to tune out all the distractions around us—the baby crying in the row in front of us, the worship team member who's singing off key, the growl in our stomach, our plans for tomorrow. That's hard sometimes, especially if we haven't had a chance to settle our spirit ahead of time. And then we have to tune in to God. If we could read the minds of those around us, we'd no doubt find questions like these: *Am I supposed to visualize God? Is that even biblical? How do I "tune in" to Him? How come those people on the stage look so mystical and I feel so, uh, normal?* We're really glad no one can read *our* mind.

This would be a good time to look at a second meaning of worship, one that was around long before we began inserting a "time of praise and worship" into our services. This second definition of worship means giving honor and reverence to God. Sounds easier, but it involves more—much more. Paul calls it a "living sacrifice" in Romans 12:1. In other words, we have to sacrifice ourselves, but it won't kill us.

So how do we give honor and reverence to God without ceasing? By developing a lifestyle of worship, one in which our entire being— everything that we do and say and think—is consecrated to Him. That means living in the moment, fully aware of Him and what He is doing in our lives as we go about our daily business. It means sharpening our spiritual sensitivity to His leading—at home, at work, in the grocery store, at the beach, in six lanes of traffic congestion. But mainly, it means keeping God as the central focus of our lives.

"It is in the process of being worshiped that God communicates His presence to men," C.S. Lewis wrote in *The Case for Christianity.* He's right, of course. People who say they've never sensed the presence of the Lord have often never quieted their minds or their spirits long enough to truly worship God. The Lord Himself told us to "be still and know that I am God" (Psalm 46:10). Hush up, He says; stop all this mental activity and focus your attention—your entire being—on Me.

That's worship. When we've learned to do that, when we've reached a place where God is central to all that we do, then we can know Him.

And then, the next time we're in a praise and worship service, we won't care one bit how mystical the worship team looks. We'll be seeing God and God alone.

*Worship the LORD
with gladness;
come before him
with joyful songs.*

Psalm 100:2

"Yet a time is
coming and has
now come when the
true worshipers will
worship the Father
in spirit and truth,
for they are the kind
of worshipers the
Father seeks."

John 4:23

No Room for Depression

Dear Darlene,

When I became a Christian, no one could have convinced me that I would eventually suffer from depression. I had found the Lord! How could I ever experience anything but the pure joy of living in His presence?

It wasn't long before I found out. Shortly afterwards, I gave birth to the first of our three children. I wanted to stay at home with them and give them the kind of Christian upbringing I hadn't had. I didn't realize how isolated I would feel, especially since my husband needed our only car to go to work.

We soon began hosting a cell group, which eliminated the problem of getting a babysitter every week. But I ended up feeling as if I had not left the house in years. I became so depressed that I hardly knew where to turn.

Like many other families, we were strapped financially, which made things even worse. But one day, after hearing "Shout to the Lord," I grabbed some of our grocery money and went right out and bought the tape.

> *How can anyone put into words what happens when the Holy Spirit moves on a person?*

How can anyone put into words what happens when the Holy Spirit moves on a person? That's what happened when I started listening to the music. I felt a deeper sense of worship than I had ever known before. Since I bought that tape, it's almost as if I have never stopped worshiping Him, no matter what I'm actually doing—even changing a diaper. My life is now centered on the Lord, and there's no longer any room in it for depression.

But let all who take refuge in you be glad; let them ever sing for joy.

Spread your protection over them, that
those who love your name may rejoice in you.

—PSALM 5:11

God's Word Is Truth

Dear Darlene,

My family has just emerged from several years of what can only be described as hell on earth. It all started with a lie, one that threatened to destroy the work resulting from my parents' decades of faithful service to God. I can't share the details, but it seemed as if my whole world was collapsing around me.

Several months before all this started, I had discovered your music. Since I had been brought up knowing the truth of God's Word, I immediately embraced the biblical truth I found in your lyrics. There was no doubt in my mind that God had inspired and anointed your music.

During our family nightmare, I realized just how anointed it was. With tears streaming down my face, I would set my CD system to "repeat play" and sing "Shout to the Lord" over and over

> *With tears streaming down my face, I would sing "Shout to the Lord" over and over again, choosing to believe the truth in those words.*

again, choosing to believe the truth in those words instead of the lies being spread about my family.

God's Word is truth, and that's what brought us through. We survived the ordeal and are stronger in the Lord than ever. Thanks for sharing your music instead of keeping it to yourself.

We also thank God continually because, when you received the word of God, which you heard from us, you accepted it not as the word of men, but as it actually is, the word of God, which is at work in you who believe.

—1 THESSALONIANS 2:13

CHAPTER 9

Shout to the Lord All the Earth, Let Us Sing Power and Majesty, Praise to the King

Come into the presence of the King! Sing and shout and proclaim His power and majesty! Let the earth and all it contains praise Him forever!

It's time to let it rip.

We cannot contain our astonishment at our Lord and King any longer. It turns out that He's everything He said He was after all. Now that is something to shout about.

Decked out in the splendor of His royal robes, the King of kings and Lord of lords holds court in our midst. If we could see His face—if we could, just for a moment, dim the light that surrounds the radiance of His glory—we would see His expression of sheer delight in those who have come into His presence.

When we enter His gates with thanksgiving and His courts with praise, the King of glory smiles.

Does His utter magnificence render you speechless? Turn once again to the book of Psalms for help, this time to Psalm 47:

"Clap your hands, all you nations;

shout to God with cries of joy.

How awesome is the LORD Most High,

the great King over all the earth!

...God has ascended amid shouts of joy,

the LORD amid the sounding of trumpets.

Sing praises to God, sing praises;

sing praises to our King, sing praises.

For God is the King of all the earth;

sing to him a psalm of praise." (v. 1-2, 5-7)

Read that out loud a few times, and you won't be at a loss for words any longer. This is where our "joyful noise" comes in. People are singing and shouting with cries of joy, trumpets are sounding, the nations are clapping their hands—and no doubt, there's some serious foot-stomping going on as well. This is one major celebration.

The church of Jesus Christ hasn't done a particularly good job of hosting a celebration in recent centuries. We can change that, and we can start by having our own celebrations—by ourselves, with our family, among our friends, at praise and worship events. The world needs to see what a real party is like, a party that begins today and continues through eternity. We need to show that the eternal party—all the singing, all the shouting, all the praising, even all the laughing—will take place only in the presence of the King.

That's the way it is in the Kingdom of Heaven, where our true allegiance as believers must lie. The Lord alone is our mighty King, the

One who reigns over us in mercy and justice in this life, and in never-ending glory in the life to come. Can we possibly praise Him too much? Pleading guilty to that accusation would be an honor indeed.

Go ahead: Shout to the Lord!

*All the earth bows
down to you;
they sing praise to
you, they sing praise
to your name.*

Psalm 66:4

Then I heard every
creature in heaven and
on earth and under the
earth and on the sea,
and all that is in them,
singing: "To him who
sits on the throne and
to the Lamb be praise
and honor and glory
and power, for
ever and ever!"

Revelation 5:13

Leading in Worship

Dear Darlene,

I can't remember a time when I didn't love to sing. When I was twelve I prayed and asked Jesus to help me sing for His glory. Over the years, the praise and worship music at church touched me in such a beautiful and special way that I often dreamed of leading the worship team.

Shortly after I bought one of your CDs, a friend of mine was killed in a car accident. We had just graduated from high school, and I couldn't believe she was gone. The one thing that got me through was Jesus. I would stay in my room and enter into the presence of the Lord as I worshiped him through the music from Hillsong. The love of God in your voice helped me to focus on the Lord again.

Eventually I was also able to dream again, imagining myself leading worship at church.

That was several years ago, and now I'm a regular member of the praise and worship team at our church. I've even had the chance to lead! Nothing makes me happier than to look out at the congregation and see people genuinely worshiping the Lord.

> *The love of God in your voice helped me to focus on the Lord again.*

> *Lift up your heads, O gates, and be lifted up, O ancient doors, that the King of glory may come in!*

—PSALM 24:7 NASB

Singing to Him

Dear Darlene,

As the choir director at our church, I had often struggled with the fact that so many of our praise and worship songs were about God while so few were directed toward Him. It was possible to sing during an entire service without ever actually communing with God.

I've always believed that the Lord inhabits the praises of His people and that He delights in our worship. But we have to give Him the opportunity to do that. I was thrilled when I discovered the music Hillsong produces, because it allows for such an opportunity.

Recently our church held a special "Night of Praise," and at the end of the service the choir led the congregation in singing "Let the Peace of God Reign" and "Shout to the Lord." The Spirit of the Lord came over me in a way that I had never experienced Him before. My personal heart for worship, as well as our church's understanding of worship, will never be the same.

> So many of our praise and worship songs were about God while so few were directed toward Him. It was possible to sing during an entire service without ever actually communing with God.

Thank you for daring to be transparent in your lyrics and for challenging believers to develop an intimate relationship with the Lord. May the Lord continue to fill you with the songs written by His own heart.

> *And do not get drunk with wine, for that is dissipation, but be filled with the Spirit, speaking to one another in psalms and hymns and spiritual songs, singing and making melody with your heart to the Lord.*
>
> —EPHESIANS 5:18-19 NASB

CHAPTER 10

Mountains Bow Down and the Seas Will Roar At the Sound of Your Name

Talk about power! We like to sing and testify about the power inherent in the name of Jesus, but we seldom stop to visualize the effects of such an indescribably strong force. We'd have a hard enough time imagining a hillock bending at the sound of His name, let alone Mount Everest.

The Bible, though, is filled with imagery that reveals the awesome power that God holds not only over the earth but also over the entire universe. Here's a sampling just from the book of Job—and it's just an introduction to the marvels of God.

He moves mountains, without their even knowing it.

He shakes the earth and makes it tremble.

He speaks to the sun, and it stops shining.

He turns off the light of the stars.

His voice thunders with a majestic roar.

He shows the waves where to stop and tells the morning when to wake.

He sends lightning bolts to their destination.

Pretty impressive, wouldn't you say? We sometimes focus so much on the tender mercies and the Father heart and the endless love of God that we conveniently forget the utter havoc and devastation He could inflict if He wanted to. The laws of the universe, which science holds to be so sacred, are mere playthings in His hands.

This might be an appropriate time to stop and thank God for withholding His wrath.

Despite the frequency of hurricanes and tornadoes, earthquakes and floods, God demonstrates His patience with rebellious human beings—believers and unbelievers alike—by keeping everything operating on an amazingly even keel. Think about it: How much patience do you have with your children when they blatantly disobey even your most reasonable rules? Now think what would happen if you really could make a volcano erupt instead of just acting like one that's about to blow.

How can He put up with people? *Why* does He put up with people? We love to point our finger at the idolaters and the adulterers and the liars and cheaters and assorted other scoundrels who behave as if they can get away with living outside God's laws. If not for *us*, we reason, the Lord would hurl a gigantic fireball at the earth and be done with the whole mess in one justified act of vengeance.

Hold it. We're people too, remember? And God loves the idolaters and all their wicked cohorts just as much as He loves us. We have nothing in the world to do with preserving His patience. In fact, we probably try His patience even more than the ungodly do, because we who claim to love the Lord ought to know better than to test His goodness and mercy by flagrantly disregarding His laws.

What if He did unleash His wrath? Could we have the peace of mind in the midst of His fury that the psalmist describes? Look at his words in Psalm 46:2: "Therefore we will not fear, though the earth give way and the mountains fall into the heart of the sea, though its waters roar and foam and the mountains quake with their surging." Some of us would have headed for the hills at the first tremor, only to discover, of course, that the hills were about to make a beeline for the bottom of the sea.

No, we have the greatest protection anyone could ask for, and it's not to be found on hills or in caves or at the summit of the highest mountain. It's only found in the abiding, unshakable love of God.

"'Though the mountains be shaken and the hills be removed, yet my unfailing love for you will not be shaken nor my covenant of peace be removed,' says the LORD, who has compassion on you" (Isaiah 54:10). That should be reassurance enough for all of us.

*Therefore we will not
fear, though the earth
give way and the
mountains fall into the
heart of the sea,
though its waters roar
and foam and the
mountains quake with
their surging.*

Psalm 46:2,3

*Therefore God
exalted him to
the highest place
and gave him the
name that is above
every name.*

Philippians 2:9

He Sees You

At five feet and no inches, Tracy always had to fight for whatever it was she wanted. But no matter what she tried to achieve, she always ended up in second place—never first, never the one to be singled out. Her fighting spirit even spilled over into her spiritual life; since God had millions of worshipers all around the world, Tracy felt she had to praise just a little bit louder, serve Him just a little bit harder, and pray just a little bit more to get Him to notice her.

One night as she waited with hundreds of other people for the doors to open before a Hillsong praise concert, Tracy became determined that nobody was going to stop her from sitting up front. God was going to see her, no matter what she had to do. Once inside, her plan worked—for about five minutes.

As she sat with her husband on their choice front-row seats, she learned that her pastor and his wife were sitting all the way in the back. *They should have gotten here early like I did*, she thought. *I fought for this seat—it's mine!* But she knew what she had to do. She sent her husband back to offer their seats to the other couple, secretly hoping they'd decline. Thirty seconds later, there they were, laying claim to her treasured seats.

> *"I raised my hands high and shouted, 'I'm here God! Please see me!'"*

Not only did Tracy end up in the second row from the back, she was also stuck behind a guy at least six feet tall! She couldn't even see the monitors above the stage. Sensing her distress, Tracy's husband reminded her that God would meet her no matter where she was; her relationship with Him was not about *where* she was but *Whose* she is.

"Everyone was praising God—including the six-foot-tall man in front of me," Tracy says. "I realized I had to fight the devil for my special time with God. I raised my hands high and shouted, 'I'm here God! Please see me!' I closed my eyes and heard God say that He saw me— that He was looking right at me. My spirit jumped! When I finally opened my eyes, my neck and collar were soaked from the tears!"

For Tracy, the praise and worship event turned into a genuine praise and worship experience. She learned that worship is a way of life and not a momentary feel-good emotion. Ever since, she has lived a life of seeking God's wonderful presence, worshiping Him in every circumstance.

God will meet us anywhere. He knows His children. We don't have to try to get God to see us, no matter how small we think we are.

I call on you, O God, for you will answer me; give ear to me and hear my prayer. Show the wonder of your great love...Keep me as the apple of your eye.

—PSALM 17:6-8

CHAPTER 11

I Sing for Joy at the Works of Your Hands

The incredible works of the hands of God—how can we ever begin to describe them? Mere words fall short. Even our singing for joy lacks words at times; our spirit takes off, leaving our mind—still groping around in the limitations of language—far, far behind.

There's no limit to what we can sing about, though. As busy as God's hands were at Creation, they are just as busy today at the work of restoration. To fail to see that is to miss seeing God as the active, personal Being He is. He is both Creator and Restorer.

Our Creator. The way Paul sees it, we have no excuse for not believing in God and all that He is. Creation itself clearly reveals God, His power, and His nature; Paul states this so matter-of-factly in Romans 1:20 that it seems not to occur to him that anyone would argue the point. Some people do, though. Many who deny God's existence can look at a spectacular sunset and see nothing more than the effects of radiation waves and atmospheric gases and microscopic particulates, even if they've never heard those terms. In other words, they see science, whether they call it that or not.

But those of us who believe in God as Creator, and still have some sense of wonder in us, gaze at the Grand Canyon, the night sky, the Pacific Ocean and ask: *How can anyone* not *believe that God did all this?*

And if we have even the least shred of romance left in our being, we sing for joy, if not with our lungs then at least with our spirit.

It is relatively easy for us to praise the Creator for these jaw-dropping marvels, but we should remember that we do fall victim to selective wonder at times. The creative works of God's hands include a host of things we really wish He hadn't made: cockroaches, mosquitoes, rattlesnakes, slugs, scorpions. Singing for joy at *those* works is probably best left to their predators. But still...they really are incredible creations, no matter how frightening or annoying or repulsive they appear to be.

Which brings us to our fellow man. The same God who "created the heavens and stretched them out, who spread out the earth and its offspring" also "gives breath to the people on it and spirit to those who walk in it" (Isaiah 42:5 NASB).

Do we see the hand of God in *people*? Of course we do—in people we love or like or feel some sense of compassion for. How about an arrogant, trash-talking NBA player? A murderous, self-righteous foreign dictator? A thieving, heartless scam artist? When we learn to see everyone as God sees them— weak, sin-soaked human beings in need of the Savior— then our heart will begin to sing from a place so deep inside us that we're astonished to discover it. Yes, we realize at last, we can love the unlovely.

Our Restorer. God's restorative works are nothing short of mind-boggling. The lame walk, the blind see, the dead come to life. You've never witnessed those miracles firsthand? Then how about these: A couple on the brink of divorce renews their vows instead. A supposedly barren woman discovers she's pregnant. A passerby rescues a newborn baby left for dead in a gutter.

Or how about this one: A heart of stone— *our* heart of stone—becomes soft and malleable in the hands of our heavenly Father.

These are wondrous works indeed, no less spectacular than a painted sky at sundown. And they are cause for singing and shouting and all manner of rejoicing.

For you make me
glad by your deeds,
O LORD; I sing
for joy at the works of
your hands.

Psalm 92:4

In the beginning,
O Lord, you laid
the foundations of
the earth, and the
heavens are the work
of your hands.

Hebrews 1:10

The Past Is Past

For ten years, Cindy's family attended the church where her father served as an elder and frequently delivered the sermon. Life seemed to be progressing pretty normally until the unthinkable happened: Cindy's father left to start a new life with another woman.

The entire family was devastated. Angry, embarrassed, and humiliated, they left the church and did not attempt to find another. Cindy in particular blamed the pastor, who had actually been one of the few people who had tried to talk some sense into her father. In her frame of mind, though, she couldn't see that. All she could see was pain.

Eventually Cindy found comfort in the arms of a man who allowed her to escape from the reality she needed to face. Her family relationships suffered, as did her relationship with the Lord. Meanwhile, her sister and brother had become reconciled to the church and often asked her to attend services with them. She always refused. Then, a friend of hers who attended the same church begged her

> *The work of God's hands created this new me, and I can't stop singing for joy about it.*

to go. Worn down by the constant requests, Cindy relented.

"I ended up having the greatest experience of my life," says Cindy. "My pastor prayed for me, and I will never forget his words: 'The past is past.' It's over. I had to start living for now, for today."

God changed Cindy's life that day. She broke up with her boyfriend and is still trying to repair the damage she allowed him to do to her. With God's help, love, and strength, Cindy got through the worst of the transition to her new life. And although she had pushed God away so often, to her amazement she discovered the God still wanted a relationship with her. She even calls Him the new man in her life, so deep is the love she now has for God.

In the year since Cindy returned to church, one song has ministered to her more than any other. "'Shout to the Lord' means so much to me," Cindy says. "'I sing for joy at the work of your hands' sums up my feelings about life. The work of God's hands created this new me, and I can't stop singing for joy about it."

The LORD *will continually guide you...and you will be like a watered garden, and like a spring of water whose waters do not fail.*

—ISAIAH 58:11 NASB

CHAPTER 12

Forever I'll Love You, Forever I'll Stand

The story of the ideal love relationship between God and His people is found in the Song of Solomon, or Song of Songs as some call it; the visual image is the picture of Jesus as the Bridegroom entering into a covenant relationship with the church, His bride. If we truly desire a deeper understanding of the kind of relationship the Lord wants with us, we have to see ourselves—individually—as the one pursued, the bride. No, this is not an image reserved for women. Once men get past the gender obstacle, they realize that they fit into this picture quite nicely.

If we could only capture this truth, the reality of the bridal love of Jesus, it would transform our lives.

But how can we do that? We can start by clarifying just how we should treat our spouse and then begin relating to Jesus in that way.

Even if we've never been married, we can list
the desired qualities of marital love:

We delight in our spouse.

We are faithful.

We give our spouse first place in our lives.

We try to please the one we've married.

We are passionate with our spouse.

We give ourselves completely to our mate.

When we look at it this way, loving Jesus
takes on a whole new dimension. *This* is a
way of loving that we can relate to. It's divine
love defined in human terms—another
specialty of God.

Secure in our newfound love relationship,
we can now stand firm in our faith. And we
can stand joyfully, not at the rigid attention
that accompanies legalism. No, now we are

finally free. And that freedom is another paradox of our life with Christ. In our spiritual union with Christ, we have the freedom that comes from knowing we are loved, unconditionally and eternally.

If that's difficult to comprehend, think in earthly terms again. If you knew, with absolute certainty, that your spouse would love you passionately and cherish you forever, would always be faithful, and would always have your best interests at heart, wouldn't you feel free?

"Your Maker is your husband," the Bible tells us in Isaiah 54:5. And with that awareness in our heart, we *can* stand firm in our faith forever.

I will sing of the LORD's great love forever; with my mouth I will make your faithfulness known through all generations. I will declare that your love stands firm forever, that you established your faithfulness in heaven itself.

Psalm 89:1, 2

*We love because he
first loved us.*

1 John 4:19

The Long Way Home

As Peter prepared for an East Coast business trip, his brother called with news that would dramatically alter the tone of that Mother's Day weekend: Greg and his wife, Emily, had just lost a perfectly normal baby girl due to an unusual set of complications during childbirth. But God seemed to have set the stage for this unexpected turn of events, as Peter was already scheduled to fly out the following morning—to Baltimore, where Greg and Emily lived.

Peter flew to the city on Sunday and immediately went to the hospital to be with his brother and sister-in-law. With no other family in the area, Greg and Emily treasured his presence that day on what should have been a joyous occasion for them. The three prayed and cried and grieved and talked about the little girl, whom they had named Juliet. Later in the day, members of their church began to show

their support for the young
couple, helping to ease their
pain even more.

> *As they drove around together during the darkest time in their marriage, Greg and Emily found that they could also stand together in the face of tragedy by drawing on the eternal love of God.*

Back in his hotel room,
Peter called home and asked
his wife, Suzanne, to fly to
Baltimore and help out while
he attended to business in Washington for
several days. He had one specific request: Bring
their Hillsong CDs, which he thought might
minister to Greg and Emily. If nothing else, he
knew the CDs would comfort him.

As anyone who has shared Greg and Emily's
experience knows, one of the most difficult
times in the parents' lives is the moment when
they have to go home *without* a baby after going
to the hospital expecting a normal delivery.
Anticipating this, Suzanne programmed the CD
player in the couple's car to play several specific
songs on the *Shout to the Lord* disc as they drove

home. Suzanne drove to their house in a separate car.

Soon after arriving at their home, Suzanne received a phone call from Greg indicating that they were not coming directly home. They had begun listening to the music, and it had ministered to them in such a profound way that they decided to drive around a bit longer so they could listen to more of it.

God had used the music and lyrics to offer comfort, hope, and peace to this grieving couple. As they drove around together during the darkest time in their marriage, Greg and Emily found that they could also stand together in the face of tragedy by drawing on the eternal love of God.

I would have lost heart,
unless I had believed

That I would see the goodness of the
LORD

In the land of the living.

—PSALM 27:13 NKJV

CHAPTER 13

Nothing Compares to the Promise I Have in You

In His perfect timing, God fulfills every promise He makes. Throughout the Old Testament, as various writers recounted the history of God's chosen people—often to bolster the sagging faith of the multitudes—they made one point over and over again: *These were the promises of God, and this is how He fulfilled them. He has never failed us in the past, and because of that, we know He will not fail us now.*

What were the promises of God? Peace, prosperity, protection, safe passage, and victory, just to name a few. Line them end to end, pile them one on top of another, group them together any way you like, and still, even collectively, they pale in comparison to the Promise—singular.

The Promise: Jesus Christ, the Son of God, leaving His throne in heaven, coming to earth as a human being to show mankind how to get to where He had just come from. Rejected, beaten, burdened with the sin of the world as He hung on a cross. Killed so we might have an abundant life on earth. Resurrected so we could have eternal life with Him in heaven. The Promise, reduced to a few words, so familiar to us that our eyes glide right across the page, scarcely allowing us a chance to take in the meaning of what we've read.

If that's too familiar, maybe we should turn our attention to the least familiar element of the Promise: eternal life. For most of us, eternal life means an odd mix of fear and relief. We're really afraid to go through the dying part, but won't it be a relief when it's all over! No one's ever come back from eternal life to tell us what it's like, though, so we decide to dig a little deeper to see if we can find out just what we've gotten ourselves into.

We read about heaven—streets of pure gold and pearls the size of city gates and a foundation made of precious stones, including something called jacinth. We don't know what that is, but it's, well, precious so it must be OK. We keep reading and find that a river runs through the main street and the kings on earth bring their splendor along with them and the servants have something written on their foreheads. Suddenly we're not so sure about all this. But God created it and promised it to us, so it must be good. And we know we're going to live there, sooner or later; the Old Testament writers have convinced us of that: *He has never failed us in the past, and because of that, we know He will not fail us now.* It's just that it all sounds so …unusual.

We close our Bibles and clear our minds. Slowly a smile begins to spread across our face and seep into our spirit. *It's all going to be all right*, we think, *because Jesus will be there.* Jesus, the essence of the Promise. He will be there, with arms outstretched, ready and waiting to greet us as we take one last deep breath, regain our strength, and sprint to the finish line.

Who cares about pearls or kings or rivers or servants? Or jacinth? Or ...how unusual it all is? Jesus will be there! Jesus, the One who made life on earth bearable, worthwhile, even joyful. The One whose tender, unfathomable love changed everything for us.

The promise we have in Him is *Him*. And nothing compares to that.

*My eyes stay open
through the watches
of the night, that
I may meditate
on your promises.*

Psalm 119:148

His divine power has given us everything we need for life and godliness through our knowledge of him who called us by his own glory and goodness. Through these he has given us his very great and precious promises...

2 Peter 1:3

Change in Plans

When Jim was just an infant, his father publicly dedicated his son's life to the ministry. As a teenager, Jim was upset that someone else had tried to determine his fate, so he rejected any attempt to steer him toward a future in ministry and decided on a military career instead.

When he learned he had been accepted to the U.S. Military Academy, Jim figured his career choice was set in stone. Even so, he never lost his love for Jesus, and at a conference for Christian college students, he made a commitment to enter the ministry—a commitment that he soon forgot all about.

Following graduation from West Point, Jim served for several years in Europe and began to put his military training to good use by planning out the next twenty years of his life. He was going to see the world as an officer, get all that he could out of life, and end his military career at the State Department. Then, and only then, would he consider attending seminary.

Jim sensed God saying to him, "You must be willing to give up your dreams for Me."

During one of his trips home, Jim spent some time with an old friend who wanted Jim to hear a tape that had ministered to him in a profound way. "When I hear this song," he told Jim, "it brings tears to my eyes." He proceeded to play "Shout to the Lord." Never had a song touched Jim spiritually as that one did. He began to rethink his plans. *It's been so long since I've heard praise like that*, he though. *If I could spend the rest of my life playing my guitar and praising God, I would be happy.*

During his time with the Lord the following morning, Jim sensed God saying to him, "You must be willing to give up your dreams for Me."

He did, and he has never looked back. He has since left the military and applied to seminary, and is now on his way toward fulfilling the commitment to ministry that his father had dedicated him to so many years before. Jim now knows where true joy in life comes from—the incomparable promises of God.

For I know the plans I have for you, says the Lord. They are plans for good and not for evil, to give you a future and a hope. In those days when you pray, I will listen. You will find me when you seek me, if you look for me in earnest. Yes, says the Lord, I will be found by you.

—JEREMIAH 29:11-14 TLB

CHAPTER 14

Write Your Own "Shouts"

The description reads like a travel brochure: Pure spring water—lush, tropical plants—palm trees—vineyards—beautiful mountain scenery. En-Gedi was a vacation destination, especially in the winter when those who lived in the open plains could escape the harsh, blowing winds and enjoy warm breezes and cool water.

But David was not in En-Gedi for a vacation. He was on the run from the man he had loyally served for many years. He—David, anointed by Samuel to be Israel's king—was hiding in a cave as Saul looked to kill him.

David did not know why Saul was so obsessed with killing him. Hadn't he slain Goliath, winning victory for Saul and all of Israel? Hadn't he been a faithful husband to Saul's daughter? Wasn't he a great source of comfort when Saul would sink into depression? David would play his harp in such a beautiful manner that Saul would relax and his despair would lift.

David wished he had his harp with him now. Even if he did, however, he could not risk the noise of playing it in the cave. So David expressed his feelings to God in another, quieter way. He began to sing—softly, in a barely audible voice—a song he was composing on the spot. Later he would have it written down. For now, he simply allowed it to pour forth from his heart.

I cry out loudly to God,
loudly I plead with God for mercy.
I spill out all my complaints
before him,
and spell out my troubles in detail:
"As I sink in despair,
my spirit ebbing away,
you know how I'm feeling,
Know the danger I'm in,
the traps hidden in my path.
Look right, look left—
there's not a soul who cares
what happens!
I'm up against it, with no exit—
bereft, left alone.

I cry out, God, call out:
'You're my last chance, my only
hope for life!'
Oh listen, please listen;
I've never been this low.
Rescue me from those who are
hunting me down;
I'm no match for them.
Get me out of this dungeon
so I can thank you in public.
Your people will form a
circle around me
and you'll bring me showers
of blessing!"

(Psalm 142, The Message)

There were no record stores when David wrote this song, no CD clubs, no radio stations playing all praise songs. The audience for this song was probably quite small when David first composed it—perhaps just him, his followers, and God. But David did not write his songs to please an earthly audience. He *had* to write these songs—they poured out of his heart with fervor. And we are the beneficiaries of his passionate cry to God. We can recite this psalm aloud when we are in our caves, surrounded by enemies and situations beyond our control.

David wrote many songs from his heart. Some came when he was in distress (along with Psalm 142, read Psalms 3, 54, and 63). Some came when he was reflecting on the awesome power of God (Psalms 18, 29, 66, 91, and 144). He wrote a song about his days spent tending a flock of sheep, comparing God with a great shepherd (Psalm 23). He wrote a song of confession following an incredible period of abuse of authority, adultery, and murder (Psalm 51). David wrote songs for every occasion, in every occasion.

You, too, can be a songwriter. Your songs may never be published. A musical score may never accompany them. They may not be recorded and sold on CDs. But when they come from your heart, they have heavenly appeal. Imagine what could happen if your wrote your own "shouts" to the Lord in a journal. If you are going through a period of great victory, write your thoughts of the greatness of God. Then, when you go through a time of great trial, reread your song to remind yourself that God is a victorious God. He will not leave you in this trial forever.

If David had not formed his heart cries into song lyrics, and then written them down, we would not have the comfort of the book of Psalms today. Your words may only bring comfort to yourself, but you never know. Perhaps God will use your "shouts" to help others in need. Perhaps, one day, your song will be sung around the world, proclaiming the greatness of our God.

On a Personal Note . . .

It is with a very grateful and overwhelmed heart I sit and write this to you.

I could never have dreamed or imagined the impact of "Shout to the Lord" around the world. No one could have convinced me or ever prepared me for the road that I have found myself traveling. This is a simple, heartfelt song of worship to Jesus Christ, my Savior and best friend, who found me and rescued me at a time when I had totally lost my grip on the reality of living in covenant relationship with Christ as a chosen daughter of the King.

Such is the incomprehensible love of our Father toward us. In Matthew 6:33, He promises that if we seek first the Kingdom of God and His righteous-ness, *all* these things will be added unto us. Is it any wonder that we find ourselves caught up in praise of Him? The more we understand Him, the more we rejoice in all that He is!

I believe that one of the reasons "Shout to the Lord" is embraced by people of all races, ages, and denominations is that it reflects the strong but sincere cry inside each human heart, a longing to be reconciled into divine relationship with our Lord and King and to put Him above all else.

His name and His word are more powerful than anything that could ever happen in your life. So my friend, *Shout to the Lord!* Live to make His praise glorious and His message alive and radiant in you! As you worship in Spirit and in truth, be very mindful that nothing compares to the promise you have in Jesus.

My love always,
Darlene

SHOUT TO THE LORD

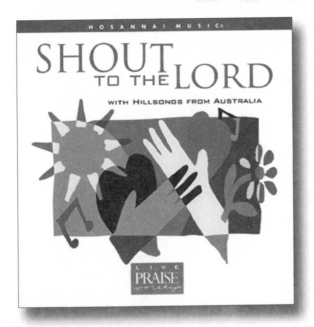

This recording captures the worship at the Hills Christian Life Center
in Sydney, Australia. Established in 1982 by Pastor Brian Houston,
this congregation is renowned for its energetic approach to worship
and practical, down-to-earth, Bible-based teaching of life principles.
As the worship leader, Darlene Zschech leads an enthusiastic
congregation of over 1500 worshipers on a journey to the throne of
our King with inspiring songs like "This Kingdom" and the
title cut, "Shout to the Lord."

This album has touched millions and has become a
best-seller throughout the world.

SHOUT TO THE LORD
2000

God's grace has touched the Hills Christian Life Centre and once again they've shared it with the rest of the world. Worship leader Darlene Zschech is joined by Alvin Slaughter and Ron Kenoly in a worship event that will propel us into the next millennium.

Recorded live during the '98 Hillsong Conference, this album captures the excitement for the future God has planned for us. This project will be cherished by those who loved the original *Shout To The Lord*. Lift your voice to greater heights with this dynamic praise and worship team.

you are my world

All Things Are Possible

Darlene Zschech

A live recording from Hillsong Music Australia including songs like "All Things Are Possible," "The Love Of God Can Do," "Love You So Much," "So Close," "Lord Of All," I Know It," and "I Live To Know You."